ROBERT SCHUMANN'S ADVI⸺ ⸺⸺⸻ MUSICIANS
REVISITED BY STEVEN ISSERLIS

Steven Isserlis enjoys a unique and multifaceted career as soloist, chamber musician and educator. He appears regularly with the world's leading orchestras, gives recitals every season in major musical centres, devises chamber music programmes, performs with many period-instrument ensembles, plays and writes for children, and works with many living composers. He has written two children's books, and gives masterclasses worldwide. For the past eighteen years he has been Artistic Director of the International Musicians' Seminar in Prussia Cove, Cornwall.

Further praise for *Robert Schumann's Advice to Young Musicians*:

'Beautifully turned and succinctly expressed.' Jessica Duchen

'This is a book which wears its learning and wisdom lightly, and makes a charming and informative read. It should be essential reading for music lovers everywhere.' *A World of Classical Music*

'The cellist Steven Isserlis revisits the romantic composer's miniclassic and adds his own wise and delightful commentary.' *Washington Post*

Robert Schumann's
Advice to Young Musicians

Revisited by

STEVEN ISSERLIS

FABER & FABER

First published in 2016
by Faber & Faber Ltd
Bloomsbury House
74–77 Great Russell Street
London WC1B 3DA

This paperback edition first published in 2020

Typeset by Faber & Faber Ltd
Printed in the UK by CPI Group (UK) Ltd, Croydon, CR0 4YY

The quote on p. 51 appears courtesy of Python (Monty) Pictures Limited

A CIP record for this book
is available from the British Library

ISBN 978-0-571-35568-6

FSC
www.fsc.org
MIX
Paper | Supporting
responsible forestry
FSC® C013604

8 10 9 7

To Joanna, with love

Contents

Introduction

In addition to being a genius – as well as the kindest of men – Robert Schumann was a phenomenon. He was astonishingly far ahead of his time, in many different ways. His music anticipated a whole multitude of trends that would spread in the 150 years after his death; almost every major composer who followed him acknowledged his influence. As a man as well as an artist the extent of his enlightenment was extraordinary. One of the most lovable ways in which he showed a new path was in his attitude to children and youth. His music for children is perhaps the most popular music of its type ever written. His music *about* childhood – *Kinderszenen*, for instance – is equally magical. His empathy with the young came from deep within; the composer and author Cyril Scott, writing in the early 1930s, described Schumann as 'the true poet of the child-soul', going so far as to claim that it was the influence of his attitude to children that brought about 'that deeper love and understanding of the child, which . . . is such a pronounced characteristic of the age'.

Schumann's concern with education didn't stop with children; he was equally concerned with the well-being of aspiring young musicians. He taught at Mendelssohn's new Conservatory in Leipzig – perhaps not entirely successfully, since teachers such as Schumann who rarely utter a word to anyone and spend most of their life in a dream-world of their own tend not to be the most helpful in practical matters; but he also wrote, more famously and successfully, a book of *Advice to Young Musicians*. This was originally intended as a companion for his celebrated books of piano pieces for children and students, *Album for the Young*, but in the end was published separately, some years later. I have always loved this book – as I love all of Schumann's writings. Alas, as the years go by, it seems to be read less and less, its high-flown language and ideals apparently unsuited to today's Internet age.

And yet – it's *not* unsuited! Schumann's poetic words of wisdom have just as much to teach us now as they did when they were first written, over 150 years ago. Perhaps, though, they need a little explanation and adaptation for a generation tempted at every moment by the dangers (as well as the pleasures) of recordings and videos that spoon-feed us with other people's interpretations rather than allowing us to find our own voices. So that's where this version of the book comes in. I have selected almost all of Schumann's pearls (the remainder can be found in the appendix), reordered them, categorised them, and tried to clarify them for today's young musicians.* As Schumann put it when describing a text commentary he'd

---

* The original can (and should) be seen online, or bought in book form, either in German, or in various English translations – including the deliciously quaint 1860 version by Henry Hugo Pierson which served (loosely) as the basis for my own translation. (Many thanks to my sister Rachel and her family for their help with translating from the Schumann.)

written himself, 'I have added some signposts, to keep people from straying.'

In general, Schumann is writing specifically for keyboard-playing young composers. I think that his advice can be useful for any musician, and also for listeners; so I have tried to extend the reach of his suggestions to include all music-lovers. I hope that my emendations and additions are not sacrilegious. It is certainly not a question of trying to 'improve' on Schumann – what a thought! I merely wish to bring the Master's thoughts to a new generation; and also (more egotistically) to experience the thrill of seeing my name displayed as co-author with the magical name of my hero of heroes.

I have also added some thoughts of my own, increasing the overall total (not exactly in line with inflation, but it's something) by ten per cent, from Schumann's original seventy to seventy-seven. In fact, with the appendix, the total is eighty-eight – the number of keys on a standard modern piano. I have the feeling that Schumann would have enjoyed that little detail.

So here we go: a series of poetic ruminations from an immortal (Schumann) brought down to earth by additions from an ordinary mortal (me). I hope that they're helpful – and even fun . . .

ON BEING A MUSICIAN

*From a pound of iron, which costs virtually nothing, a
thousand watch-springs can be made, which are worth a
fortune. That pound, which you have received from the
Lord – use it faithfully.*

Schumann himself doesn't start with this nugget – but I feel
that it's a good place to begin. Is any child born unmusi-
cal? I think not. Every infant, given the chance, will enjoy
fun rhythms and catchy tunes, almost from birth; that's why
we have nursery rhymes. From then on, though, each child's
relationship with music will develop in a unique way. Alas,
only a small proportion will get a chance to study it properly
– such a pity, when the benefits of a musical education are so
unarguably documented. And of those who have the chance
to study music, only a few will choose to make it their profession. But that's fine – we need many more listeners than
performers!

   As to the pound of iron that we've been handed: there's no
denying that the Lord has endowed some people with more
natural musical aptitude than others; but that's no reason
for the less talented ones to be discouraged. In fact, talent

can be a danger; all too many young musicians abuse their gifts, rather than 'using them faithfully'. For some of them, it can all feel just too easy, with the result that they get lazy, and end up being superficial performers. Those who have to work harder can often develop more interestingly. As for those who feel that they really have *no* talent for playing or singing – don't give up! The more you engage with music, on whatever level, the better you will understand it; and the more you understand, the more you will get out of it. Hopefully, your studies will give you a love for music that will enrich your whole life. If not, it's probably because you've been taught badly. For those who've decided that they hate music because their piano teacher Miss Smith rapped them on the knuckles when they played a wrong note, I'd say: give music another chance! It's not Beethoven's fault that Miss Smith was an old sourpuss. Nor yours – and you're the one who'll miss out if you cut music out of your life.

Nothing great can be achieved in art without enthusiasm.

Yes – what's the point in even trying to be a musician if you don't love, love, LOVE music with all your heart? Great music is the best possible friend one could have: it will be with you in times of happiness and of sadness; and it will never let you down or abandon you. Why would we *not* be enthusiastic? Having said which, I have to admit that there is a big difference between music itself and the music profession. Some aspects of the latter are likely to drive you mad at times, if you're part of it. That makes it all the more important, then, to remember why we wanted to be musicians in the first place: because music lives in our hearts. And we have to keep it there.

*Through diligent study and perseverance you will rise
ever higher.*

That's obvious, really; but it still needs to be said. I've seen
very gifted young performers fade away because they've become self-satisfied and stopped developing. What makes one
grow as a musician is as much as anything else a constant
feeling of dissatisfaction – rather like the irritation in an oys-
ter that produces a pearl. That doesn't mean to say that we
have to be neurotically self-critical, always unhappy with any
performance we give; it just means that we have always to aim
higher. Of course we will never reach the level that reigns in
our imaginations; but we have to keep trying. After all, even
the greatest composers felt that their music could have been
better. If Beethoven wasn't satisfied with himself, we can't be
satisfied with ourselves either. Back to work . . .

The laws of morals are those of art.

What the great man is saying here (I think) is that there is good music and bad music – as well as good and bad interpretations. The greatest music, even if it's tragic in nature, takes us to a world more elevated than ours; somehow the beauty, the profundity uplifts us. Bad music, on the other hand, degrades us. It's the same with performances: a bad performance isn't necessarily the result of incompetence. Some of the worst travesties occur when the performers, no matter how accomplished, are thinking more of themselves than of the music they're playing. These doubtful characters aren't really listening to what the composer is saying – they're just showing off, hoping that they'll have a great 'success' with the public. The performer's basic task is to try to understand the meaning of the music, and then to communicate it honestly to others. Simple, really . . . (well, perhaps not always *that* simple!).

*Never miss an opportunity to play music with others; as
for example in Duets, Trios, etc. This will give you
a flowing and lively style of playing. Also accompany
singers often.*

That's an interesting way of putting it. I'd add that not only does playing chamber music give you 'a flowing and lively style of playing': rather more vitally, it teaches you to *listen*, perhaps the most important skill of all. For listen we must, at all times – to the composer, and to our fellow musicians. It's not enough to try to squeeze every little drop out of every note in our own part, in order to be noticed; that's rather like a footballer who gets possession of the ball and keeps it as long as he possibly can, refusing to pass it even though that ruins his team's chances of scoring – ridiculous. In fact, I'd say that *all* music is chamber music, and needs to be treated as such, whether it be a concerto, a symphony, a piece for small ensemble, or even a solo piece; there is always a dialogue between voices, which is the essence of chamber music. And it is up to us to balance those voices, to bring out the conversation. (I was born lucky, in that my two older sisters were already playing instruments by the time I took up the cello. We played together almost from the beginning; and the life of a little brother who ignores what his sisters are doing really isn't worth living. So I learned to pay attention to other voices . . .)

As to accompanying singers: yes, that is very important – and not just for pianists. But as Schumann himself tactfully puts it:

*You can learn quite a lot from singers, but
do not believe all that they say!*

Ahem – well, yes. Perhaps not *all* operatic tenors, for example, have been among the greatest intellects on the planet; and one cannot usually imitate a singer on an instrument (easier for them to imitate an instrument, probably). But one can learn much about legato, about articulation, about breathing, about *talking* through one's instrument, from them. From the good ones, that is. And one can also learn about intonation. A good singer will never use piano intonation; intervals will be altered by microtones in order to increase or decrease their intensity. The same should be true for string and wind players; expressive intonation is an essential part of interpretation.

Never miss good operas.

It's very important to get to know operas (as long as you can afford the tickets – thankfully, though, that situation seems to be getting better all the time). It's revealing to see how composers treat words and dramatic situations in their music; Mozart's operas, for instance, give one strong clues as to what he is expressing in much of his instrumental music. Besides, good opera productions can be overwhelmingly wonderful – although, it must be admitted, bad ones can be torture . . .

Frequently sing in choruses, especially the middle parts;
this will help to make you into a real musician.

It's a good idea to sing in a chorus – even if, like me, you sound like a corncrake with a mulberry stuck in his beak. It's very useful to feel how a singer phrases and breathes from personal experience, as well as getting to know wonderful choral music. And if you're a singer, I'd recommend playing a stringed instrument, so that you can see how the other half bows. Meanwhile, *all* musicians should be able to play the piano – at least well enough to study their pieces from the score or from a piano reduction.

If you are endowed with a good voice, do not hesitate to cultivate it – consider it the most valuable gift that heaven has granted you!

I wouldn't know from personal experience . . . but he's right, of course (as always).

If everybody were to play first violin, we could not have an orchestra. Therefore respect each musician in his own place.

A real pearl of wisdom, this one. Not everybody is going to be a soloist. Many people understand this, and are content to play in an orchestra or chamber group, or to teach; these musicians are every bit as vital as those whose names may become better known. But there will always be those for whom the glittering career is all-important; these are usually the least interesting interpreters – and that way bitterness lies, because even if they do achieve outward success, they'll feel empty inside. Many of the greatest musicians I have known have been primarily teachers rather than performers; without these teachers there would be no performers, anyway. (Schumann himself wrote at one point: 'I want to become a real piano teacher, and compose in addition.') And many of the most knowledgeable, perceptive musicians I know play in orchestras or chamber groups, or sing in choruses. We have to find our own niche, our proper place, in the music world, as in any other profession; what matters most is that we use our love of music to enhance our own lives and the lives of others.

The object of art is not to acquire wealth. Become a great artist, and other things will come.

Ah, so right, so right – though few of us object to riches, if truth be told. But if earning a lot of money is your principal aim as a classical musician, then you're in the wrong profession. (Try managing a hedge fund instead.) The same goes for applause: it's lovely, and I don't know of any musician who does not enjoy an enthusiastic reception (even if they pretend not to); but it must not be the main goal. An honest approach to music will not necessarily whip an audience into a frenzy (depending on the piece); it may leave them in thoughtful mode. But people with true sensitivity to music will feel your sincerity and be moved by it; and moving people is more important than impressing them.

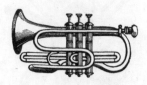

Make sure that your head is not turned by the applause of the crowd, often accorded to so-called 'great virtuosi'; that of artists is of greater value.

Yes – so often one goes to a concert, sees a performer showing off horribly, and the audience reacts with fevered enthusiasm. It's hard not to be depressed by this. It means nothing, though; that sort of triumph is hollow. If you have a big success, by all means enjoy it – that is only human. But remember that it's not the main thing; the applause won't last for long. (Schumann rather rudely compared audiences to a herd of cattle momentarily distracted from its grazing by a flash of lightning.) Later, when you are alone, think back over your performance; and also ask the opinion of honest friends whom you can trust – Schumann's 'artists' – because intelligent feedback is important. Then decide whether you really deserved the accolades. Remember that there's *always* room for improvement – and artistic growth.

When you play, don't worry about who may be listening to you.

Well – unless they happen to be artists, presumably? (See p. 20.) Again, though, what he's reminding us here is that our relationship to the music should be stronger than our relationship to the public.

*Never help to popularise bad compositions;
on the contrary, do your best to suppress them.
You should neither play bad compositions, nor,
unless compelled, listen to them.*

This can be awkward; if a composer writes a piece for you, you may feel obliged to perform it, even if you don't like it. You can usually avoid playing it for a second time, though, if you explain to the composer (as gently as possible) that you don't really feel that you can do justice to the piece. As for listening to bad compositions: the way in which music surrounds us now is completely different from anything Schumann could have imagined. What would he have made of the Muzak that assaults our ears almost every time we leave our homes? He'd have gone mad. (Well, yes – he did that anyway, I know; but his last years would have been yet more tragic and awful if they'd had piped music in his asylum.) Leaving Muzak aside, though, it's tricky to avoid hearing bad music on a fairly regular basis – there's so much of it about! If one's stuck in a concert hall or opera house, walking out is usually not an option – it's too embarrassing; but try to avoid repeating the experience if you can. Choose your musical encounters carefully; make sure they fan, and don't quench, the flames of your love for music.

On the other hand, choosing isn't always that simple:

Do not judge a composition from a first hearing; that
which appeals to you at an initial encounter is not always
the best. The works of the masters need to be studied. Many
things will not become clear to you till you have reached a
more advanced age.

Hmm . . . so how is one to know for certain on a first hearing
whether a work is good or bad? Perhaps if the piece is by a
composer one knows to be great, one should give it the bene-
fit of the doubt; if it doesn't speak to you on a first hearing, try
again – we lesser beings are more likely to be mistaken than
the immortals. For many years, for example, I just couldn't
understand the First Cello Sonata of Gabriel Fauré, one of
my favourite composers. So I worked at it, and worked at it;
and then, suddenly, it was if I'd gone through a door, and the
music made perfect sense to me. The strange thing was that,
having stepped over that threshold, I then couldn't remember why I hadn't understood the sonata in the first place – it
now seemed so clear.

With composers we don't know, of course, particularly
those writing in an innovative musical language, it is more

difficult. We have to give unfamiliar music a chance, or even several chances – but not waste our lives trying to find a meaning that is not there. Ultimately, I suppose we have to trust our instincts. These are *essential* in music; losing touch with your musical intuition is fatal. One can educate instincts, certainly – but never ignore them.

When you are older, do not play fashionable stuff. Time is precious. All that is merely fashionable will soon become old-fashioned; and if you keep playing these works, you will become known as a charlatan whom nobody respects.

A charlatan, eh? Sounds bad. I'm sure, though, that he's not telling us to play *only* the greatest, most profound music. Some lighter fare – including virtuoso pieces – can be wonderful; and some all-too-serious music can be awful. He's just advising us to stick to music that is real, not written merely for effect.

Respect the old highly, but also take a warm interest in the new. Do not be prejudiced against names unknown to you.

It's a temptation as a performer to stick to the tried and tested masterpieces, and of course the great composers are likely to be at the centre of our repertoire (if they have written for our instrument); but we must remember that there are always worthwhile lesser-known works waiting to be explored. Discovering a neglected gem is a real thrill. Also – and this is really what Schumann is emphasising – it is the *duty* of every performer to play the music of his or her own time, and if possible to commission new works. That's what keeps music alive! It is also (usually) really enjoyable to work with a living composer – and so very useful to have him/her on hand. If I have a question about a piece by a friend of mine, I can call up said friend and put the query to them; whereas every time I've tried to call Haydn or Schubert recently, they've refused to answer the phone, or to return my call. So rude.

Be sensitive to the requirements of your audience; but never play anything of which you are inwardly ashamed.

There is nothing wrong with wanting audiences to enjoy your concerts; but one should avoid 'playing down' to them. Play music that you would want to hear yourself, that genuinely speaks to you. If you truly believe in the piece that you are performing, and are able to communicate that belief, the public will respond – and will be grateful.

In judging compositions, discriminate between works of real art and those designed merely for the entertainment of amateurs.* Cherish those of the former description, and do not get angry about the others.

Here he's telling us (I think) to have strong musical values, but not to be snobs. There's a place for great music, and a place for lighter music. (Not that the two are mutually exclusive; great music is very often lots of fun too – think of Beethoven!) There's no place for bad music, though. Well, perhaps there is: the waste-paper basket. Or, these days, the recycling bin.

* Schumann uses here the expression *dilettantische Unterhaltung*, which sounds pejorative; but I'm not sure that it is – after all, he does tell us not to get angry (*erzürne*) about them.

We cannot bring up healthy children by feeding them just pastry and confectionery. As with bodily food, mental food must be simple and nourishing. Great composers have provided enough of these sorts of nutritional pieces; stick to them.

This means that if one plays lighter works – confectionery – one should make sure it's good, healthy stuff. Schumann was writing at a time when people would play really silly pieces at their concerts – most of them mercifully forgotten today; but they've been replaced by other bilge. So it's important to choose music – whether it be profound or just good fun – that has nutritional value. It's essential for one's musical health. (Maybe scales, exercises, etc., are the vitamin pills?) Anyway – point made about good and bad music; on to other matters . . .

It has been said that a perfect musician must be able to visualise even a complicated piece of orchestral music on first hearing as if it were lying before him in full score. This is indeed the greatest achievement that can be imagined.

Gulp. I'm sure that there *are* people who can do that; but I'm certainly not of their number, and I'm not sure I know anyone who is – possibly some of my composer friends might manage it. (Schumann could probably do it himself – but then, he was Schumann; and I wonder whether even he could have coped with some of the scores one hears/sees today.) We can keep trying, though. And besides, we can at least comfort ourselves with the thought that there is really no such thing as perfection in music, or 'a perfect musician'. ('Bach?' I hear you saying. 'Don't interrupt!' I hear myself replying.)

You must reach the stage where you are able to understand a piece of music, just from seeing it on paper.

That's easier – still not easy, but worth the attempt. The more you look at a score, the more you will find there; and eventually you may be able to hear pieces in your head that you've never heard outside it.

Cultivation of the ear is of the greatest importance. Try right from the beginning to distinguish each tone and key. Find out the exact notes sounded by the bell, the windowpane, the cuckoo, etc.*

Hmm . . . this is quite a challenge. I can't say I've ever really tried that with the bell or the windowpane (and it might be hard to find a cuckoo these days, at least in a city – perhaps a pigeon would do?); but I'm sure that he's got a very good point. (He usually does. No, he *always* does.) The better trained and more discerning the ear is, the more it will pick up when we are playing, singing, or listening. Incidentally, 'perfect pitch' – the ability to tell which note is being played – can be very useful, especially for sight-reading, and can apparently be acquired through training; but it's not essential – many of the greatest musicians have not had it.

---

* Schumann himself obviously considered this paragraph one of the most important, since the original book begins with it.

*Learn the fundamental principles of harmony as
soon as you can. Do not be afraid of the words theory,
thoroughbass, counterpoint, etc.; they will become your
friends if you become theirs.*

Yes, one *has* to know something about harmony and theory in
order to understand music. The great composers themselves
certainly thought (think) in those terms. But, as he says, don't
be put off by those rather intimidating words. It ought to be
enjoyable to study harmony; one can teach oneself a lot just by
looking carefully at the music of the masters. If in addition you
read the writings of musicologists, that can be helpful too – but
make sure they are the sort of writings that are useful to you.
There are some musicologists who write for normal people,
some who write only for their colleagues. The former will help
one understand the piece they are describing, and thus make
one more keenly aware of its beauties; the latter will, as it were,
point out the entrails and other internal organs – which might
be helpful to doctors of music (and possibly to composers,
though I'm not convinced of that), but much less so to the rest
of us. *Nothing* in the study of music should be dry or boring.

*You must become acquainted by degrees with all the
principal works of the important masters.*

That's hard – especially now, over 150 years since he wrote
that, when there are so many more such works. One can try
– but, reassuringly, Schumann also admits that:

*We should need to live a hundred lives just to become
acquainted with all the good works that exist.*

That's more like it; even the most knowledgeable among us
won't get to know more than a fraction of what's on offer –
not in this life, anyway. My idea of heaven is that since there'll
be no such thing as time, one will be able to get to know every
piece of music worth knowing, see every play, read every
book, etc. And eat every dish on the menu – without getting
fat!

And I'm sure that if there *is* such a thing as heaven,
Schumann is there now, feeding his insatiable curiosity by
becoming acquainted with all the good works that have ever
existed, or are ever going to exist. During his tragic last years
on earth, in the asylum, he even described himself as 'Robert
Schumann: Honorary Member of Heaven'.

As you grow up, communicate more with scores
than with virtuosi.

This is a crucial point. When you are young, you are bound to be inspired by the performances of your heroes; indeed, many people decide to take up an instrument because they idolise particular players. So it is inevitable that a certain amount of imitation will take place. But as you grow up, you have to outgrow those influences. You may still admire your heroes deeply; but it is essential to find your own musical voice. Don't listen to (or watch) anyone, no matter how wonderful, playing the pieces you are learning; just look at the score – and keep looking. You'll always notice new things there. The only person to whom a mature musician is answerable is the composer; any third party – the editor, another interpreter, etc. – is an irrelevance. Why talk to a vicar when you can talk to God?

Talking of editors: take *very* good care that the markings are the composer's own, not those of an editor. (Schumann, ahead of his time in this as in so much else, was vehement in his condemnation of bad editions.) And be warned: some so-called 'Urtext' editions, if they reflect some editor's crack-pot theories, can be as misleading as old-fashioned editions that openly change the composer's markings. Try to find copies of manuscripts and first editions if you can. You have to know *what* the composer wrote before you can understand *why* he/she wrote it.

Love your instrument, but do not be vain enough to consider it the greatest and only one. Remember that there are others as fine as yours. Remember also that singers exist, and that choral music with orchestra is the most sublime music.

Come, come – now he's going a bit far. Obviously the cello IS the greatest instrument. But good advice for non-cellists, anyway.

Ha ha.

It's so true about choral music, though – think of Bach's Passions, Beethoven's *Missa solemnis*, etc. Music doesn't get any better than that.

What does it mean to be 'musical'? You will not seem to be,
if your eyes are fixed anxiously on the notes and you toil
through your piece laboriously; or if, when somebody turns
over two pages at once, you get stuck and cannot go on.
But you will be, if you can almost predict what is to follow
in a new piece, or remember it in an old one – that is to
say, if you have music not only in your fingers, but also in
your head and heart.

Well, it's pretty clear that one can't give a convincing
performance of a piece until one knows it properly; but he
means more than that. He's saying that not only must we
know the notes, we must speak the language of the composer
whose work we are performing; and we must have mastered
the piece sufficiently to be able to *recreate* it, not just to play
it. Real technique allows us to listen as we play/sing, without
being distracted by worrying about how we're going to tackle
a particular passage; and a true knowledge of the piece we
are playing entails understanding how each note fits into the
overall shape of the work.

But how do we become 'musical'? This, my young friend,* is a gift from above; it consists chiefly of a fine ear and a quick understanding. But these gifts may be cultivated and enhanced. You will not become musical merely by shutting yourself in your room for days on end and working on mere mechanical studies, but rather by immersing yourself in the vibrant, multi-faceted musical world – especially with choirs and orchestras.

By 'immersing yourself in the music world', Schumann surely means a general knowledge of music, including familiarity with a broad range of works by the composers whose music we play, and with the music of many different periods and styles. True that musicality is to a certain extent 'a gift from above'; but that is just a beginning. We have to delve thoroughly into the works we perform, to strive constantly to understand what the composer had in mind. As for listening to choral works – that is very important, as well as rewarding; but I'd add that it is also essential for all musicians to listen to chamber music, to instrumental and orchestral works, and to the great song-cycles.

---

* Schumann writes here *Liebes Kind,* ('dear child'); but if this book is really for children, it must be for very precocious ones!

There is no end to learning.

Ah, so true. Well, until one takes one's last breath, I suppose. But even after that sad event, perhaps one will arrive at the next world, thinking, with some relief, that one has reached the end of learning; there the great composers will be, though, waiting for us, scores in hand. 'You misunderstood this!' 'Why did you change that note?' And so on – a slightly worrying thought . . .

PLAYING

If your music comes from your heart and soul, and if you feel it inside yourself, it will affect others in the same way.*

Yes: if your music comes from deep inside you, it will speak to a deep place in others. But it's not *just* heart and soul – your mind needs to be engaged too; all three should work together (in concert, as it were) in order for you either to create music or to recreate the works you interpret. There is absolutely no contradiction between thinking and feeling; it's all part of understanding.

* In the original, Schumann seems to be directing this advice chiefly towards composers; but it applies to all musicians, of course.

Do not aim for mere dexterity, or so-called 'bravura'. Try to recreate the spirit intended by the composer, nothing more; anything else is a caricature. All mechanical brilliance fades over time; technical skill is of value only when it serves a higher purpose.

In other words, don't show off at the expense of the music. Your first duty is to the composer, second to yourself, third to the audience. Of course, one needs to play virtuosic passages clearly and accurately in all sorts of music; but don't try to draw attention to your virtuosity – it will be noticed anyway (by those worth impressing, at any rate). Think beyond mechanical technique. Besides, your performance will improve in every way if you have the bigger picture in mind. I find that difficult passages become much easier to master when I am thinking in properly musical terms. For instance, a scale in octaves may be hard in itself; but if I see where it is going – towards a major structural climax, perhaps – suddenly the problem tends to be solved (or at least solvable).

Consider it an abomination to alter works of good composers, to omit parts of them, or to insert new-fashioned ornaments. This is the greatest insult you can offer to Art.

I wonder whether this was a dig at Liszt, who at one point in his career was (in)famous for superimposing trills and tremolandi on the works of other composers? Schumann's general point here, though, is that we must avoid *inappropriate* additions or alterations to the musical text. Each composer writes in his or her unique language. The music they left us is preserved in a code, which we have to crack. Some composers have left us specific instructions, which we have to follow to the letter; others, particularly in earlier periods (baroque, for instance), have left most of the interpretive decisions to us. In much baroque music it is almost essential to add ornamentation at times; composers would have expected it. As Schumann says, though, it is a lapse of taste to insert 'new-fashioned' ornaments (including unnecessary/careless vibrato, glissandi, pedalling, etc.); our additions have to enhance the music, not distort it. Every note we play must belong to the style and spirit of the work we are playing. Ideally, we should be like actors who almost *become* the characters they are portraying, with every gesture being part of that character. We have to understand why the composers wrote everything they wrote, as great actors understand the motives behind all their characters' speeches and actions. Or, to use another simile: don't take the dish that the composer has painstakingly prepared and pour sugar, cream or tomato ketchup (or all three at once) all over it.

Dragging and rushing are both major faults.

Difficult to argue with that one!

If anyone should place before you a composition to play at sight, read it over before you play it.

Or with that one either; sorry – I'm not being much help here, am I?

Endeavour, even with a poor voice, to sing at sight without the aid of your instrument; in that way your ear for music will constantly improve.

Hmm . . . how many of us actually do this? I certainly don't. (Admissions like that always remind me of that wonderful line from *Monty Python's Flying Circus*: 'How many of us can honestly say that at one time or another he hasn't set fire to some great public building? I know I have.' I wonder if Schumann would have liked *Monty Python*?) But of course singing through a piece can be a very useful exercise – even if one just does it internally.

Play strictly in time! The playing of many a virtuoso resembles the walk of a drunkard. Do not take those sorts of performances as your models.

Again, this should be obvious, really; but it is so often ignored. An overall sense of tempo, and a feeling for the natural connection between different tempi within a movement or within a whole work, are essential in almost any music; usually when a performance seems to take for ever, it's because the performers are distorting the basic rhythmic structure. And within that larger structure, one must also make sure that the smaller rhythms are properly timed. One can't merely reproduce the value of each note exactly as written – that would sound mechanical (singers would certainly never do it, unless they happen to be robots); but one has to respect the beat. If one takes time over a certain note in a group, then one generally has to give it back on the following ones, so that the larger beat is undisturbed (i.e. *rubato* – 'robbed time' – or the so-called 'agogic accent'). Too many musicians ignore this cardinal rule – as they evidently did in Schumann's time as well. The result is that the music becomes unnecessarily complicated and hard to follow – and therefore becomes boring. My teacher used to have one cardinal rule: 'Thou shalt not bore.' Amen.*

* On a more practical note: when you come across a complicated rhythmic passage, an imperceptibly tapping foot can be mighty useful . . .

*Endeavour to play easy pieces well and beautifully; that is
better than playing difficult pieces badly.*

Spot on! He was rather clever, this Mr Schumann. It's not easy
to play *anything* perfectly. (I found that out to my cost when my
great friend, the pianist Stephen Hough, and I made an album
of children's pieces together. We started with a short, simple
piece that my son, Gabriel, had played pretty well when he
was seven years old. We finished the play-through, and waited
impatiently for the producer to tell us to move on to the next
piece. There was a pause, then his voice came over the speaker:
'Thank you. We just need to get rid of that scratch in bar two;
slight intonation problems on that B in bar three; there was a
squeak on the first beat of bar four.' And so on.) It's far more
satisfying to give a good performance of a so-called 'easy' piece
than a scrappy performance of a difficult one. But what is an
easy piece? Whereas a fast, fiendish-sounding movement in
a Shostakovich concerto gets easier with time, once one has
mastered the notes, the slow movement of a Beethoven sonata
demands almost as much work the fiftieth time one plays it as it
did the first time. But the rewards are (even) greater.

The spirit of a composition will not become clear to you until you understand the form.

So very, very, very true! I often ask a student who has just played me a sonata-form movement to play or sing me the three main themes of that movement; but alas – all too often, there is a deafening silence, as the student frantically searches the page for the answer. Does one read a novel without knowing who the main characters are – and without wanting to know what happens to them? It's exactly the same thing. If you don't understand the basic form of the music you're playing, you'll be like a walker groping his way through a forest; it's possible to see some pretty trees and plants, perhaps, as you walk – but, basically, you're lost. Once you understand the shape, the structure, of the piece, you are set free: then you are like a bird flying above that forest, able to enjoy the beauty as a whole, with a constant overview of your path. And for the listener as much as the player, the whole process seems to take half as long, because there is a sense of direction.

PRACTISING

Practise scales and other finger exercises diligently; but that alone is not enough. There are many people who think they can obtain great results in this way, and who spend many hours in such mechanical labour every day, right into old age. That is the equivalent of trying to pronounce the alphabet faster every day! You can employ your time more usefully.

Yes: the bad news is that one really does have to do some scales and exercises every day, just to discipline the fingers (or voice); but the good news is that it really shouldn't take too long – they are merely a means to a far more enjoyable end. We always have to know *why* we're doing them. Some people are tempted to think that if they're suffering in their practice, they must be doing themselves good; but that's a dangerous fallacy. I think of the scale and exercise routine with which I start each practice day as cleaning my cellistic teeth; I quite enjoy it, in fact – partly because it only takes about ten minutes. My fingers become reacquainted with the cello and the bow; and then I'm ready to start my real, creative work. Some people have gained a certain facility, I suppose, from endless scales and studies; but that's not the same as acquiring a great technique. Genuine technical command allows us to play the music we're performing without having to think about the difficulties; it gives us the freedom to listen to ourselves. The point of scales and exercises, ultimately, is to help our fingers/voices acquire the precision they need in order to produce the interpretation we hear in our heads/hearts.

Play always as if in the presence of a master.

There is a lot behind this simple sentence. How would practising in the presence of a master affect our work? Well, for a start, we wouldn't drift off and dream of other things as we played; or stop every five minutes to check our email, or whatever. (I'm all too guilty of the latter offence – but then, I'm not setting myself up as an example. I'm writing this book because I need to profit from Schumann's wise advice as much as any other reader!) There is no point in practising without concentration, without a specific aim in mind; playing through a piece badly several times will do far more harm than good – it will merely reinforce bad habits, and make them harder to expunge. Assuming that the anonymous master hasn't time to sit there listening to us practise, however, we have to become our own masters, asking ourselves *why* we are repeating a passage, what was wrong with it before, and what it is that we are aiming to improve. The really good thing about this is that if we don't just repeat aimlessly, but focus on what really needs to be done, then our practice is likely to be finished far sooner; and we can go away and deal with those dreams and messages . . .

*When you have done your musical day's work and feel
tired, do not exert yourself further. It is better to rest than
to work without pleasure and vigour.*

We like this one, don't we? Mr Schumann is right, as ever;
don't torture yourself! Just do what has to be done that day,
as efficiently as you can – and then go and do something else.
It's a good idea to give yourself a programme: 'I have to practise this, and this and this'; and then when you've finished
working on those tasks, you may justly feel that you deserve
a rest. Then, if you want to stay with music, you can listen
to a work you don't know, perhaps, or study a score. But,
believe it or not, you can also do something completely different. There *are* other things in life, surprising though that
may seem to some fanatics.

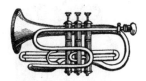

*Relieve the severity of your musical studies by reading
poetry. Take lots of walks!*

For example. I do feel, though, that Schumann had in mind
a more serious type of young musician than we usually find
today. Not that I disagree in any way with his ideas of reading poetry or taking walks. It is important (as well as hugely
satisfying and uplifting) to be generally cultured – to be well
read, and appreciative of all the arts; and needless to say one
has to look after one's health, and enjoy the inexhaustible
beauties of nature. But, for most of us, there are also TV
shows to be watched, Internet sites to be explored, gossip
to be spread, etc. We need to have fun! That's where I feel
that we have rather departed from Schumann's world. Des-
pite his frequent references in letters to his 'humour' (and
there's certainly plenty of it in his music), I do doubt whether
Schumann was ever really silly; and I can't quite imagine him
sitting down to play a video game, or cheering on his local
soccer team. But perhaps I'm doing him an injustice; after all,
his favourite drink was apparently champagne mixed with
beer (yuk) – so perhaps he wasn't *that* super-cultured . . .

*Never tinkle away! Always play with energy – and
do not play a piece half-heartedly.*

Basically – concentrate!

* There is some controversy about what Schumann means here. He writes
Spiele immer frisch zu, und nie ein Stück halb! My German-speaking friends
are divided about it. It seems to mean either: 'Don't play half a piece'; or
'don't play a piece with half-energy'. The latter seems more apt to me.

Take care always to have your instrument well tuned.

Well, yes: it will be much more pleasant – for you, and for anyone else within earshot.

*It is not only your fingers that should know your pieces;
you should also be able to hum them away from your
instrument.* Sharpen your imagination to the extent that
you remember not only the melody of a composition, but
also the harmony that belongs to it.*

This is not just about memory; it's really about getting to
know a work away from our own instrument. It is vital that
our interpretation should come from our imaginations, not
from our fingers. Too many performances are shaped by
what feels physically comfortable, rather than by what the
music truly requires. You should tell your fingers what to do,
not the other way around! (Even if there are ten of them, and
only one of you.)

Studying the music without our instrument – at the piano,
perhaps, if you're not a pianist – should constitute a fair proportion of our practice time. We *have* to know the whole of
a score in order to understand any piece of music. Learning
just our own part makes no more sense than an actor getting

* Schumann writes 'piano'.

to know one part in a play, without having any idea of what the other characters are saying or doing. And as for remembering 'not only the melody of a composition, but also the harmony that surrounds it': that is equally crucial. A melody needs its harmony as a head needs its body.

COMPOSING[*]

* Also see p. 45.

It is certainly very nice for you to make up little melodies at the piano; but if they come to you on their own, away from the piano, then you can be even happier, since that means that an inner feeling for music is stirring within you. The fingers must do what the head desires; not the contrary.

So – keep composing, even when you're doing the washing-up, lying in bed, counting goats or whatever.

If you are starting out on a composition, begin by working everything out in your head. Do not try out a piece on your instrument until you have fully conceived it in your mind.

That's quite a challenge; but all he's pointing out (again) is that it shouldn't be the fingers that are the composers, any more than they should be the interpreters (see above) – it should be the mind. Mozart would sit at convivial dinners in a complete daze, contributing nothing to the conversation, because he was busy composing in his head. After dinner, when his friends had left, he would sit down and write out the music he'd composed; as he wrote, he'd ask his wife to repeat the conversation, so that he could catch up on what he'd missed. Notating the piece was a purely mechanical task for him, not requiring any concentration; he'd already done all the work in his mind.

If Heaven has bestowed on you a fine imagination, you will often spend your solitary hours seated spellbound at the piano; you will want to express the feelings of your heart in harmony, and the more elusive the sphere of harmony may perhaps be to you, the more mysteriously you will feel as if you are being drawn into a magic circle. In youth these may be your happiest hours. Beware, however, of abandoning yourself too often to the influence of a talent that induces you to lavish your powers and time upon phantoms. Mastery over the forms of composition and a clear expression of your ideas can be attained only by constant writing. Write, therefore, more than you improvise.

This feels autobiographical. We know that the young Schumann spent countless hours at his beloved piano; his genius probably began to manifest itself there. But as he confessed to Hummel in an early letter: 'The fact that I sat at the piano all day and improvised proves nothing.' There's a difference between playing whatever comes into your head and real composing. (We're not talking about jazz here, by the way – that's something else altogether.) Beethoven's improvisations were said to have been extraordinary and unique, and probably gave him invaluable new ideas; but that doesn't mean that he could have improvised his great works. Some of his later pieces took him several years to complete, in fact, each note hewn with huge effort; one can feel that in the seeming inevitability, the extraordinary depth of the music. The same goes for speech. People can give wonderful speeches off the cuff, of course; but a Shakespeare play, with its layers of meanings and hidden connections, had to be written down and worked upon with infinite care in order to attain the profound universality that has spoken to generation after generation.

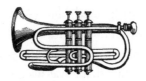

Get to know the tone and character of the various instruments as soon as you can; try to impress their unique tone-colours on your ear. Also get to know the range of the human voice, in its four main types. Listen to these voices, especially in choirs; discover in which intervals their greatest strength lies, and which others can be used to produce soft and tender effects.

Yes, that's essential for a composer – not just to learn what's physically possible, but to find out what really suits the nature of the different instruments and voices; how to balance them; when to stretch the possibilities; when to compromise so that the player or singer doesn't have to struggle in a way that ends up ruining the music; and so on. Understand your materials!

I do think that it's important not to torture your performers needlessly; remember that some things *are* impossible. On the other hand, it's also important to know when to insist on having it your own way. The first cellist to try to play Schumann's Cello Concerto insisted that the last movement was unplayable, and told him that he must rewrite it; thank goodness Schumann ignored him. (A similar tale, rather closer to home: when Thomas Adès sent me the last movement of his *Lieux retrouvés* for cello and piano, I sent him a furious email telling him that it was just too difficult, that he would have to rewrite it completely, and that was that. Back came a very nice, apologetic reply, saying that he was very sorry, he was sure it was his fault, and that we could cancel the premiere with no shame, putting it down to his cello writing; someone else would perform it later. That did it – someone else do the premiere? Perish the thought! Back I ran to the cello; and somehow I found a way around the difficulties. And I'm very glad that I did. Hmm . . . maybe I shouldn't tell that story?)

Listen attentively to folksongs; they contain a treasure-trove of the finest melodies, and afford you an insight into the character of the different nations.

Interesting advice, that; so many great composers of the twentieth century took their inspiration from folk music. As usual, Schumann was looking into the future.

Provide yourself as soon as you can with a knowledge of the art of conducting. Observe the best conductors often, and conduct along with them in your mind, where you are in control. This will provide you with clarity.

This is important both for composers and for instrumentalists/singers. For the latter, whether or not you intend eventually to become a conductor yourself, it will give you a clear idea of what is or is not likely to work when you are being accompanied by an orchestra; and if you are going to play within an orchestra, it may give you a little more sympathy with the conductor's plight! For the former, it's doubly useful to study conducting – not just for the practicalities of orchestral writing, but also because if you can conduct your music yourself (well, that is), your conception is more likely to be realised in a way that will satisfy you. And if you're like Stravinsky, you'll also see the advantage of being paid both as composer and as performer.

*Remember, there are other people in the world besides yourself.**

Be modest! You have not yet invented nor thought of anything that someone else has not thought of or invented before. And should you really have done so, consider it as a gift from above, which you must share with others. Studying the history of music and hearing live performances of masterpieces from different periods will be the quickest cure for vanity or conceit.

I wonder if Schumann was really writing this one for himself? Perhaps trying to keep his own ego in check, since he really *did* invent music that had not even been dreamed of before; perhaps that was almost frightening for him in some way. Anyway, I'm very happy that he considered it a gift that he was obliged to share with others. As for hearing live performances of masterpieces (for Schumann, of course, the *only* way to hear music was to attend a live performance; I

* Schumann uses the rather lovely expression here: *Hinter den Bergen wohnen auch Leute* – literally, 'Other people live behind the mountain.'

presume that he would also allow us to listen to recordings – preferably score in hand): I'm sure that one can learn more by getting to know great works than through any other form of study. I think it's fair to say that every major composer has been steeped in the music of the past, and has developed from it, either by growing from it organically or by reacting against it – or both.

Perhaps genius alone understands genius fully.

Oh dear. That's bad news. Oh well – the rest of us can but do our best . . .

MY OWN BITS OF ADVICE
(FOR WHAT THEY'RE WORTH)

On Being a Musician

The most important thing as you enter the musical profession is to vow NEVER to lose your love for the music itself. That may sound obvious; but actually, it can be a challenge. You'll encounter people who really don't understand the language of music talking complete nonsense about it, with great authority (on the surface, at least); others believe them, and start repeating the same nonsense. It's the sheep syndrome: once one of them starts bleating, the whole flock joins in. It can be unsettling; a little voice inside you is bound to ask: 'Can so many people really be wrong?' Furthermore, no matter how successful you are, you have to be prepared to face repeated rejection in the course of your career; it will feel personal, and it will hurt. So you need to have strong convictions, and courage, in order to maintain your artistic faith. But as long as you remember that it is the music and the composers who belong at the centre of your artistic life, rather than those others, and have the strength never to forget that core truth – then a life in music can be the best, most deeply privileged, of all lives.

～

Avoid pretension: we have our tasks as musicians, just as other professionals do. But also – don't be cynical; it's *not* just an office job. Music is the language of the gods, surely; we who spend our lives with it are blessed (even if it doesn't always feel like it – at a morning rehearsal, for instance).

~

Don't spend too much time talking about your career! Unfortunately, there are some young musicians whose idea of a good evening is to spend hours telling their fellow students (who have dreams and ambitions of their own too, of course) all about what they're going to do with their professional lives, what good reviews they've had recently, etc. Avoid it – nobody but you really cares. (Well, perhaps your parents do too – but that can be a poisoned chalice . . .)

~

Talking of reviews: if you get to a point at which people are writing about your performances or your compositions, you have to take a deep breath, and maintain a clear sense of proportion. Most musicians read their reviews, whether they admit it or not; and most are upset by them. Some writers, if you're lucky, will be intelligent and understanding; others will not. You'll have given a performance that seems to have been warmly received, and you're happy about it; and then you'll read a report that shows that the critic has totally misunderstood everything you've been trying to do – and if he or she has missed the point, you'll wonder, does that mean that other listeners have too? There's no answer to that question; the best method of coping is to remember that Bach, Mozart, Beethoven, Schubert, etc., all suffered the same fate. It's part of the whole caboodle of being a musician, and we just have to lump it. *C'est la vie.* And there are, and have been, some truly perceptive critics – including one who was probably the great-est of them all: Robert Schumann.

~

By all means find out about the composers' lives, and read their letters, because it will make you feel closer to them (and anyway, it's so enjoyable – the great composers were such fascinating characters); but don't let that rule your interpre-tation of their works. It can be a danger – people read about Shostakovich's political troubles, for instance, and end up over-emphasising his irony and bitterness at the expense of the very real tenderness and poetry in much of his music. Similarly, inventing stories for the pieces you are playing can be useful – for some pieces, anyway; but be careful not to let that story take over your interpretation. The composer may well not have been thinking along the same lines. The music will change for you every time you play it; listen to what it is telling you – don't tell it what to say.

~

Remember that joy and humour are as important as tragedy in the music of most of the great composers.

~

Don't overestimate the importance of beauty for its own sake. Many people can make a more-or-less beautiful sound; but *truth* is what we should be seeking, with beauty almost as a by-product. It's the same as speech: very nice if you have a good speaking voice – but it's what you say that matters. Simi-larly, beware of becoming a 'projection-junkie'. Be aware that your audience has to hear your performance clearly, of course; but don't become obsessed with being as loud as possible at all times. If an actor were to stride to the front of the stage and yell out the speech 'To be or not to be' at the top of his voice, no doubt people would hear every word; but they wouldn't hear the meaning.

~

Try above all to understand what each composer is trying to communicate to us through their instructions, as well as their notes. Composers can have quite dissimilar meanings in mind when they use the same terms: a *pianissimo* in Schubert, for instance, tends to be very distinct from a *pianissimo* in Beethoven. And markings such as *sf*, *fp* and so on have wide-ranging connotations for each composer and each period. Sometimes *sf* is stronger than *fp*, sometimes it's the other way round; sometimes *fp* implies that one plays *piano* after it, sometimes it's just a form of accent that doesn't really affect the overall dynamic; and so on. Similarly with articulation: dots, dashes, slurs and the like have different meanings for different music, and also for different instruments. It is part of our calling to be aware of, and to understand, the significance of all these indications. Why has the composer written them? And similarly: we have to understand, if a phrase is varied when it's repeated, why this is, and what effect the changes have on the character of the phrase. Music is full of clues that the composer has left for us; our task is to investigate them. A musician has to be a detective, in fact!

~

It is a strange paradox that musicians who adhere closely to the score will sound utterly different from each other, whereas those who don't tend to sound similar. That is usually because the latter have learned the pieces more from recordings than from the music itself, whereas the former have reached their own individual conclusions. But never try to sound different just for the sake of it; you *are* different. The composer has a unique message for you; you just have to receive and transmit it faithfully. Don't 'do' things to the music – let it speak for itself; then it will do things to you.

~

Contour　A composer may write the same sort of accents several times in a row during the course of a few bars; but that doesn't mean that they are to be played with the same weight. Equal accents can kill a phrase. Make sure that every line you play – with or without hairpins or dynamics – has contour; loud passages contain softer notes, just as soft passages incorporate stronger ones. (Also – remember that loud and soft are not just a matter of volume; strong articulation in a *piano* passage, for instance, can give the impression of *forte*.) Listen carefully to how you speak, how your voice shapes words and sentences; you'll find that no two syllables are exactly alike. Music is the same: each note has its purpose, its place; it is either going somewhere or coming away from somewhere – or arriving, in which case it is the central point. Every phrase or clause has one of these latter: pivotal notes around which the others swarm – the queen bees of notes, in fact. But make sure that you select just one for each phrase or clause: too many queen bees, and the line will collapse in a sticky mess.

~

Phrase-lengths   In most eighteenth- and much nineteenth-century music, four-bar phrases or clauses are the norm; in fact, we seem to be hard-wired to feel them naturally. So when a composer inserts a three-bar or five-bar phrase into a classically formed structure, it is usually a deliberate confounding of aural expectations, and we have to be conscious of it. We also have to be aware of where each phrase begins and ends, and where it needs to breathe. These points are the equivalents of punctuation in written language: commas, semicolons, full stops, etc. – they all occur in music. And we must also be sensitive to metric accents – whether the first beat of a bar is emphasised or whether the stress contradicts the bar line. Schumann's rhythms are wonderfully imaginative; if we misinterpret or ignore his subtleties, however, we can make the music sound four-square (significant expression!) – the very opposite of the truth.

~

Performance practice   People are far more interested now in the history of performance styles than they were in Schumann's time (although Schumann himself was very interested in ancient music: he programmed the works of Clari, Palestrina and many other 'ancient' composers with his choir in Dresden). These days we have almost as many 'period-instrument' groups as modern-instrument ones; and it is very important to understand what these instruments, and written evidence revealing how music was performed in the past, can teach us. Read treatises from various eras; even if they frequently contradict each other, they are always instructive. We have to learn as much as we can about the shorthand and playing/ singing styles of different periods in music. There are times when ignoring contemporary conventions is simply a mistake: playing a rhythmic figure as written instead of double-dotting it in certain baroque pieces, for instance, or emphasising the second note of a two-note slur, can be like pronouncing the 'e' in 'blue'. But approach historical evidence imaginatively: if a writer urges performers not to play in a certain way, for example, that means that they *were* playing in that way at the time. So what is 'authentic'?

~

Anyway – having done your homework, don't turn your performances into lecture-recitals! How many times does someone play Bach, for instance, and we hear from their playing what they've learned about double-dotting, ornamentation, etc.; and we also hear that they know when the music is changing key, because they take time over every modulation. And so? We don't want to know how clever you are – we just want to hear the piece. The music will modulate whether you point it out or not; you just have to *understand* the harmonies, and make them clear through your phrasing and colours – no more. Ideally, there should be no sense that you've made decisions in advance – more the impression that you are (re)creating as you perform. That way, the music you play will always sound alive – and new.

Playing

Planning a programme: if it's up to you to plan a programme – a recital, for instance – you have to choose it very carefully. What you play or sing matters almost as much as how you play or sing. What sort of audience do you want to attract? If you stick exclusively to famous works, you are in danger of attracting people who are interested only in hearing pieces that they already know, and may not be listening very attentively. They might be the sort who find classical music 'relaxing'. (Grrr . . . whoever says that the theatre is just 'relaxing'? And is there any less drama, any narrower range of emotions, in music than in theatre? There certainly shouldn't be.) Also, if you play only established masterpieces, you may be in danger of seeming arrogant: 'I'm young, but I have something new to say about this music.' That may be true – but it's a risk. On the other hand, if you play only new or unknown pieces, you may be branded as a 'specialist'. Perhaps that is fine, if you want to concentrate on a certain type of music, as some do; but it is not a decision to be made lightly. Each artist will form his or her own audience. In general (but it really is a generalisation) I would recommend building programmes of genuine exploration, blending the familiar with the unfamiliar, with some points of connection between them. That way you can introduce novelties to people who would not normally come across them; in time, your audience will learn to trust you, and to know that if you choose to play a piece, it's because it's worth hearing.

~

Don't have unrealistic expectations of yourself. We all try to do our best – but nobody can do better than that. The term 'technical perfection' is bandied about quite a lot; it's meaningless. Technical perfection would mean not just playing all the right notes, but shaping each note precisely as it should be shaped, executing the music exactly as we hear it in our heads. It's simply not possible. Note-perfect accuracy is something different; but that sort of precision has its dangers. The less involved you are with the music, the easier it may be to play all the right notes; but what's truly 'right' about an uninvolved performance? A concert should involve a certain amount of risk. And if you come to make a recording: remember that perfection is not possible here either. A recording is like a photograph of the way one played a certain work on a particular day – with just the most obvious blemishes (which don't matter in a live performance, but would be distracting on repeated listening) removed from the photograph.

~

If you're playing music written in a particular ethnic style – Jewish or Hungarian, for instance – don't exaggerate. Play in the spirit that the music truly suggests to you; don't imitate something you've heard elsewhere. As with 'historically informed' performances (see above) the style must come from the music itself, and from your inner reaction to it – not from an outside source.

~

A pet peeve of mine   Something that I think is extremely important for performers on wind or string instruments (except when you're in an orchestra) is to avoid tuning on stage, unless it's an emergency. That may sound like a minor gripe – but actually, it's not. So many concerts are ruined before they start by the performer walking on stage, and then making a horrible noise as he or she fusses (usually unnecessarily) with the tuning. You've spoiled the experience before you start. If you're playing with a keyboard, get the A from backstage. Then you can walk on and take your listeners straight into the magical world of music. (And remember that pressure from the bow or breath can alter intonation quite a bit, if your instrument does go slightly out of tune.) Even more vital: don't tune between movements unless it's a matter of life and death. (And if it is, tune quietly!) The tonal relationships between movements are fundamental; they are ruined if unrelated tones (open strings, for instance) assail our poor ears. I was once at a performance of Schubert's great String Quintet. The first movement ends darkly in C; and then, astonishingly, the slow movement opens in E – as if we have been ushered through a gate to heaven. It should be miraculous. On this occasion, one of the players started tuning his strings immediately the first movement ended; so unfortunately I was forced to go on stage and hold him upside down by his toes until he went blue in the face. It did rather spoil the atmosphere of the performance, perhaps – but no more than his tuning had spoiled it already. (OK – so that last bit of the story is not strictly true; but I've been tempted . . .)

~

The silences in music are as important as the notes.

Practising

Even if you know a piece of music from memory, from time to time practise it with the music in front of you. Each dynamic, articulation, tempo marking conveys an important message from the composer to us. It's almost impossible to remember each little indication; we need reminding – and being reminded will put those markings in a different light. The great composers have something new to say to us every time we talk with them.

~

Practise calmly – don't panic! There's no point in getting angry with yourself as you practise; that could end in disaster (as it did for me once when I was a boy: in my frustration, I slammed the cello down on the floor, and broke it – one of the worst days of my life). If something isn't working, your task is to isolate the problem, and fix it. Similarly, there's not much point in working yourself up into a musical passion as you practise; you probably won't learn much, even if you have a good time. On the whole, practice should be an objective ex-perience – enjoyable in a quiet way. If it's boring (as inevitably it will be sometimes, even though it shouldn't be) it's because your brain isn't engaged enough. It's true that your muscles can do a certain amount by themselves, some of which can be useful (if they're doing it correctly); but the real pleasure of practice lies in engaging in a creative dialogue with the music, and thus getting closer to it.

~

The balance between playing through pieces and practising them in detail can be tricky. This problem can be solved to a certain extent if you're able to play regularly with other people, in which case you'll probably have to play through large sections, if not whole movements; if you don't have that possibility, though, it's even more essential to get the balance right. Taking music apart endlessly can divorce you from its essence; you need to play through pieces from time to time, even if you hear yourself making mistakes while you do so. On the other hand, playing through pieces carelessly time after time is damaging – faults become ingrained. Similarly, one has to get the balance of when and how much to practise. If you're ill, of course, you're excused (especially if you're a singer); but on the other hand, if we were to practise only when we really felt like it, most of us would never practise at all. (As a parent, one faces the same tricky equation: it is essential to persuade your child to work properly, while at the same time not putting them off for life. When I was a little boy, my parents used to make me practise for an hour a day after school. I protested, of course; but they insisted. 'Some day you'll thank us,' they would say primly. And annoyingly – I do!) We musicians shouldn't be obsessive in our work habits; but we have to be disciplined. And if we really don't want to practise, but know that we must, it's worth remembering that other people are spending their whole lives doing jobs that they hate and detest; we're the lucky ones.

Composing

I'm really not sure that I should be giving any advice to composers, since I'm not one myself. But as a player, I've worked with a large variety of composers: some who write in so-called 'contemporary' language, some who deliberately hark back to the past, some who mix all sorts of different languages; some who know exactly how they want each note to be played, some who really haven't a clue; some who understand the cello brilliantly, some who write chords that are physically impossible to play; and so on. The most important thing for me, though, is to feel that there is an individual, genuine voice, expressing something that the composer really means to say. The music has to be *true*. And, of course, skilled and structured – basically the same criteria that we apply to interpreters, in fact. If the piece seems to be a success on its first outing, that's nice; but it's never predictable, nor is it any proof that the success will endure. A standing ovation won't last (people have to sit down eventually); great music will. Find your own unique voice by studying the voices of the past (both distant and recent), and then moving beyond that into your own world. It will take time – there's no way of forcing it; but I'm convinced that it is the only road to greatness.

∼

And finally, one other little nugget of doubtful wisdom, with which many may disagree: don't think that in order to be profound you have always to be dark and depressing. True, terrible things happen in our world, and the music of our time is likely to reflect that in some way. But terrible things have always happened in the world – as I write this book, in fact, although these times are undoubtedly scary, much of the world is in better condition than it was a hundred years ago. And nature is still beautiful: sunsets are as stunning as ever, mountains are still awe-inspiring, the sea is still wild, and so on. Of course, write as you feel, and try to move beyond mere entertainment (unless that's all you're aiming for); but don't think that you are necessarily being superficial if your works fail to cast their listeners down into a pit of gloom. Fauré felt that the ultimate purpose of music – of all art, in fact, but particularly music – was 'to lift us as far as possible above what is'. Perhaps he was right. And if we interpreters are servants to the composer, it's also true that most, if not all, great composers felt that they too were serving a higher force . . .

Appendix

Schumann was writing specifically for pianist/composers, operating (I feel) in a very different world from ours. I have omitted, or partially omitted, a few of his seventy paragraphs (in addition to fusing some together and separating others), because I felt either that they no longer quite applied to our world, or that they were aimed solely at keyboard players. But who am I to edit Schumann? So here are the rest of his aphorisms . . .

~

Somebody has invented a so-called 'dummy keyboard';
try one for a while, and you will discover that they are
useless. Dumb people cannot teach us to speak.

I wonder what he'd have made of electric keyboards, synthesizers, etc.?

~

*When it comes to choosing which pieces to study,
ask the advice of more experienced people; that way you
will save a lot of time.*

Isn't that a bit obvious? And experience doesn't necessarily equate with wisdom. But anyway, fair enough – ask your teacher, or someone else whose opinion you respect.

~

Much playing in society is more harmful than useful.

True, but it doesn't happen often these days.

~

*Often play the fugues of good masters, above all, those by
Johann Sebastian Bach. Let his* Well-tempered Clavier
*be your daily bread. Then you will certainly become a
competent musician.*

Absolutely – but alas, we non-keyboard players find them hard. It's certainly important for every musician to get to know them, though, masterpieces that they are; and they're essential fare for keyboard players.

~

Amongst your friends, look for those who are more knowledgeable than you are.

Hmm . . . but if they do the same, who's going to be friends with whom?

~

A fine book about music is Über Reinheit der Tonkunst *('On Purity in Music'), by [Anton Friedrich Justus] Thibaut. Read it often, when you get older.*

Ah . . . I haven't; ahem. But I should, I know – it is available in English.

~

If you pass a church and hear an organ, go in and listen. If you're lucky enough to get the chance to sit on the organ bench yourself, try playing with your little fingers and be awed by the supreme power of music.

That must be wonderful; but unfortunately, not many of us get the chance.

~

Miss no opportunity to practise the organ; no other instrument reveals so clearly sloppiness in composition as well as playing.

Yes – they call it the king of instruments; and kings are usually demanding, as well as commanding. But again – we probably have fewer opportunities to play the organ today than they did then; and not many of us non-keyboard players could get much out of it anyway. Still – if you do get the chance, go for it!

~

Make sure to practise the reading of old clefs from a young age; otherwise many treasures from past times will remain closed to you.

Nowadays computers and modern editions have made us lazy; perhaps that's a pity. We should all be proficient at least in the four major clefs (treble, alto, tenor and bass); it's essential for reading a score.

~

Melody is the battle-cry of amateurs, and certainly music without melody is nothing. Be sure to understand, however, what these people mean by it: anything simply flowing, with a pleasing rhythm, is enough to satisfy them. But there are any number of different types; such masters as Bach, Mozart, Beethoven have a thousand different ways of speaking to you. Hopefully you will soon get tired of the monotonous melodies of the new Italian operas.

Again, this doesn't really apply today, with our vast panoply of musical languages; but the basic point is still valid. I do wonder what Schumann would make of some of the pop music we have today; perhaps he'd have opted to go the asylum a few years earlier! And, equally, I can hardly imagine what he'd make of the curious noises that sometimes pass for contemporary music these days. With his genius, though, he'd probably be able to distinguish the good from the bad in all musical genres.

~

Look as deeply into life as into the other arts and sciences.

Ah, so true, so true. Except that I'm not quite sure what he means . . .

Acknowledgements

Writing is never really a solo venture – especially in this case. I would like to offer my warmest thanks to my charming co-author, Herr Schumann, for being the perfect collaborator. His contributions were of course wonderfully inspiring – in fact, the initial idea for the book was his; and yet, he had the tact not to criticise my additions at all. I hope that his (characteristic) silence was an approving one.

Slightly louder, but still tactful, were several people rejoicing in the surname of Matthews: Belinda and Samantha (no relation to each other, curiously) at Fabers, and the composer Colin (who is related to Belinda, in a way – he is married to her) (and she to him, by a happy coincidence). All of them encouraged me to write this book, and then made all the right sorts of noises when I sent it to them. Michael Downes kindly checked the text for style and clarity (and gave me interesting advice about when to use 'that' and when to use 'which' – I'd always wondered). Joanna Bergin also read a draft (especially kind, since she hates draughts) and made helpful suggestions.

Finally, I'd like to thank the many, many young musicians with whom I've interacted over the years, whose generous reactions to my wise/unwise advice gave me the idea that this book might be welcomed. Time will tell whether I was right. . .